SIDE by SIDE

POEMS TO READ TOGETHER

SIDE *by* SIDE

POEMS TO READ TOGETHER

SIDE by SIDE

POEMS TO READ TOGETHER

COLLECTED BY

Lee Bennett Hopkins

ILLUSTRATED BY

Hilary Knight

A TRUMPET CLUB SPECIAL EDITION

For Fran Hoffman, lifelong friend.

LBH

For Sarah–Chris–Kathy–Matt, side by side.

HK

· INTRODUCTION ·

I recently received a letter from a child telling me how much she loved poetry; the letter ended with a P.S.: "A poem refreshes the world."

I have read many definitions of poetry by master poets and critics during the nearly three decades I have used poetry with children. None impressed me more than this gem from a youngster.

Poetry, indeed, "refreshes the world!"

Where, for example, will you find such images as rain kissing you; the sound of a stick licking a pickety fence; rabbits dancing under the moon? Nowhere—except in poetry.

Traveling throughout the country and sharing poetry with students of all ages, I have seen how poetry has enhanced the lives of children anywhere and everywhere, giving them familiar sounds and quiet music that only children continue to hear. Poetry comes naturally to those discovering the magic of language. Pictures develop inside young minds, stretching imaginations, evoking fresh visions, generating smiles, reflections, and satisfaction.

I have said it many times. I shall say it over and over again: Poetry should flow freely in the lives of children; it should come to them as naturally as breathing; for nothing—*no thing*—can ring and rage through hearts and minds as does this body of literature.

The poems in *Side by Side* are meant to be read aloud—spoken, shouted, sung, enjoyed.

You will find classic works that generations of children have heard and loved by such writers as Edward Lear,

Lewis Carroll, Robert Louis Stevenson, Kate Greenaway, Langston Hughes, Robert Frost, Harry Behn and Dorothy Aldis. More contemporary poets include Myra Cohn Livingston, David McCord, Aileen Fisher and Eve Merriam. There are newer voices as well, some being heard for the first time in this collection.

Topics in this bountiful collection include the seasons, playtime, the animal world, alphabet and counting rhymes, nighttime, and story poems.

Hilary Knight's distinguished illustrations breathe new life into the poems—illustrations that youngsters and adults will want to look at over and over again.

Sit a child on your lap, get comfortable, and side-by-side enjoy the rich experience of reading poetry aloud. I invite you to climb the "poet-tree" with me. Reach out, stretch on tip-toe; there is no limit to sharing. It will be a lifelong, lifetime gift from you to a child.

Lee Bennett Hopkins
SCARBOROUGH, NEW YORK

SIDE by SIDE

POEMS TO READ TOGETHER

SPRING

Spring Again

Spring again
Spring again
Spring again
Isn't it?
Buds on the branches
A breeze in the blue
And me without mittens
My sweater unbuttoned
A spring full of things
All before me to do.

KARLA KUSKIN

Catherine

Catherine said, "I'll think I'll bake
A most delicious chocolate cake."
She took some mud and mixed it up
While adding water from a cup
And then some weeds and nuts and bark
And special gravel from the park
A thistle and a dash of sand.
She beat out all the lumps by hand.
And on the top she wrote "To You"
The way she says the bakers do
And then she signed it "Fondly C."
And gave the whole of it to me.
I thanked her but I wouldn't dream
Of eating cake without ice cream.

KARLA KUSKIN

Tommy

I put a seed into the ground
And said, "I'll watch it grow."
I watered it and cared for it
As well as I could know.

One day I walked in my back yard,
And oh, what did I see!
My seed had popped itself right out
Without consulting me.

GWENDOLYN BROOKS

April Rain Song

Let the rain kiss you.
Let the rain beat upon your head
    with silver liquid drops.
Let the rain sing you a lullaby.

The rain makes still pools on the sidewalk.
The rain makes running pools in the gutter.
The rain plays a little sleep-song
    on our roof at night—

And I love the rain.

LANGSTON HUGHES

Rain

The rain is raining all around,
    It falls on field and tree,
It rains on the umbrellas here,
    And on the ships at sea.

ROBERT LOUIS STEVENSON

Easter's Coming

Through the sunshine,
through the shadow,
down the hillside,
down the meadow,
little streams
run bright and merry,
bursting with the news
they carry,
singing, shouting,
laughing, humming,
"Easter's coming,
Easter's coming!"

AILEEN FISHER

The Pickety Fence

The pickety fence
The pickety fence
Give it a lick it's
The pickety fence
Give it a lick it's
A clickety fence
Give it a lick it's
A lickety fence
Give it a lick
Give it a lick
Give it a lick
With a rickety stick
Pickety
Pickety
Pickety
Pick

DAVID MC CORD

PLAYTIME

Leap and Dance

The lion walks on padded paws,
The squirrel leaps from limb to limb,
While flies can crawl straight up a wall,
And seals can dive and swim.
The worm, it wiggles all around,
The monkey swings by its tail,
And birds may hop upon the ground,
Or spread their wings and sail.
But boys and girls have much more fun;
They leap and dance
And walk
And *run*.

ANONYMOUS

Follow the Leader

Follow the leader away in a row,
Into the barn and out we go,
A long slide down the hay,
Splash in a puddle, through a hedge,
And slowly up to the buzzing edge
Of a bees' hive, then run away!
Oh what a wonderful game to play!

Follow the leader on and on,
Around a tree, across a lawn,
Under the sprinkler's drifting spray,
Eat one berry, let two drop,
A somersault and a hippity-hop!
Oh what a wonderful game to play!
All over the farm on a summer day!

HARRY BEHN

The Swing

How do you like to go up in a swing,
    Up in the air so blue?
Oh, I do think it the pleasantest thing
    Ever a child can do!

Up in the air and over the wall,
    Till I can see so wide,
Rivers and trees and cattle and all
    Over the countryside—

Till I look down on the garden green,
    Down on the roof so brown—
Up in the air I go flying again,
    Up in the air and down!

ROBERT LOUIS STEVENSON

Come Out to Play

Girls and boys, come out to play,
The moon is shining bright as day.
Leave your supper, and leave your sleep,
And come with your playfellows into the street.

MOTHER GOOSE

To July

Here's to July,
Here's to July,
For the bird,
And the bee,
And the butterfly;
For the flowers
That blossom
For feasting the eye;
For skates, balls,
And jump ropes,
For swings that go high;
For rocketry
Fireworks that
Blaze in the sky,
Oh, here's to July!

ANONYMOUS

The Picnic

We brought a rug for sitting on,
Our lunch was in a box.
The sand was warm. We didn't wear
Hats or Shoes or Socks.

Waves came curling up the beach.
We waded. It was fun.
Our sandwiches were different kinds.
I dropped my jelly one.

DOROTHY ALDIS

Munching Peaches

Munching peaches in the summer,
Munching peaches cool and sweet,
Munching peaches morn to midnight,
Munching peaches. Such a treat.

Munching peaches. Munching peaches.
What a way to spend the time.

While munching,
        munching,
                munching peaches,

I had time to write this rhyme.

LEE BENNETT HOPKINS

Sea Wave

It tumbled and it crumbled
Like a mountain in a quake.
It thundered and I wondered
At the power it could make.
It trickled and it tickled me.
I saw it disappear.
The mountain was a murmuring
Of ocean in my ear.

SANDRA LIATSOS

Seaweed

Seaweed from high tide
where sand and breakers meet,
gummy
on my tummy,
slippery
on my feet.

MYRA COHN LIVINGSTON

Moonstruck

I'd like to see rabbits
under the moon,
dancing in winter,
dancing in June,
dancing around
while twilight lingers
and blinky-eyed stars
look down through their fingers.

I'd like to see rabbits
under the moon,
but I always,
always
have to go to bed too soon.

AILEEN FISHER

RABBIT
HOP
DANCE
TONIC

Birds and Beasts

Will You?

What kind of creature will you be?
Will you dig with your claws?
Will you hang from a tree?

Will you snuff at the ground?
Catch a bug for lunch?
Scratch yourself all around?

Will you crawl near the shore?
Will you snort or grunt?
Will you howl or roar?

Or will you quietly hiss
    like

        this s s s s s s s s?

EVE MERRIAM

I Went to the Animal Fair

I went to the animal fair,
The birds and beasts were there.
The big baboon by the light
   of the moon
Was combing his auburn hair.

The monkey he got drunk.
He stepped on the elephant's trunk.
The elephant sneezed
And fell on his knees,
And that was the end of the monk,
   the monk, the monk.
And that was the end
   of the monk.

ANONYMOUS

The Handiest Nose

An elephant's nose
is the handiest nose,
the handiest nose of all—
it curves and sways
in the cleverest ways,
and trumpets a bugle call;
it reaches high
in the leafy sky
for bunches of leaves to eat,
and snuffs around
all over the ground
and dusts the elephant's feet.

An elephant's nose
is the dandiest nose,
the handiest nose of all
for holding a palm,
when the day is calm,
as an elephant's parasol,
and making a spray
for a sultry day,
and a hose for sprinkling, too,
and a hand to wag
near your peanut bag
when you watch him at the zoo.

Oh, an elephant's nose
is fun to see,
an elephant's nose is fine;
it's clever as ever
a nose can be
but I'm glad it isn't *mine.*

AILEEN FISHER

The Three Little Kittens

Three little kittens lost their mittens;
  And they began to cry,
    "Oh, mother dear,
     We very much fear
That we have lost our mittens."
    "Lost your mittens!
     You naughty kittens!
Then you shall have no pie!"
      "Mee-ow, mee-ow, mee-ow."
"No, you shall have no pie."
      "Mee-ow, mee-ow, mee-ow."

The three little kittens found their mittens;
  And they began to cry,
    "Oh, mother dear,
     See here, see here!
See, we have found our mittens!"
    "Put on your mittens,
     You silly kittens,
And you shall have some pie."
      "Purr-r, purr-r, purr-r,
Oh, let us have some pie!
      Purr-r, purr-r, purr-r."

The three little kittens put on their mittens,
   And soon ate up the pie;
      "Oh, mother dear,
      We greatly fear
   That we have soiled our mittens!"
      "Soiled your mittens!
      You naughty kittens!"
   Then they began to sigh,
      "Mee-ow, mee-ow, mee-ow."
   Then they began to sigh,
      "Mee-ow, mee-ow, mee-ow."

The three little kittens washed their mittens,
   And hung them out to dry;
      "Oh, mother dear,
      Do not you hear
   That we have washed our mittens?"
      "Washed your mittens!
      Oh, you're good kittens!
   But I smell a rat close by,
      Hush, hush! Mee-ow, mee-ow"
   "We smell a rat close by,
      Mee-ow, mee-ow, mee-ow."

ELIZA LEE FOLLEN

Secret

Mrs. Kangaroo
Is it true,
Are you hiding
Someone new
In the pocket
Part of you?

There *must* be someone
New and growing,
His little ears
Have started showing.

BEVERLY MC LOUGHLAND

from
A Book of Pigericks

There was a small pig who wept tears
When his mother said, "I'll wash your ears."
As she poured on the soap,
He cried, "Oh, how I hope
This won't happen again for ten years!"

ARNOLD LOBEL

❖ 20 ❖

Grandpa Bear's Lullaby

The night is long
But fur is deep.
You will be warm
In winter sleep.

The food is gone
But dreams are sweet
And they will be
Your winter meat.

The cave is dark
But dreams are bright
And they will serve
As winter light.

Sleep, my little cubs, sleep.

JANE YOLEN

Wild Geese

When I watch
Their flock in flight
And when I hear their cries
I wonder how
They always know
Their way through
Distant skies.

SANDRA LIATSOS

FALL

Halloween

The sky was yellow,
the moon was green,
and the little old Witch
whispered:

"Halloween!"

and, at the word,
from an ivied tower
thirteen black bats
in a black bat shower
came fluttering through
the pea-green gloom
and rested there
on the WITCH'S BROOM!

(And a Witch's Broom—
pray not forget—
is a million times faster
than any JET!)
So they went to the moon,
and they circled about,
then they swept and they swept
till they swept it out;
they swept out the moon
and they made their flight—

THERE AND BACK

in a single night.

IVY O. EASTWICK

Look at That!

Look at that!
Ghosts lined up
at the laundromat,
all around the
block.

Each has
bleach
and some
detergent.

Each one seems to
think it
urgent

to take a spin
in a
washing machine

before the
clock
strikes
Halloween!

LILIAN MOORE

BLACK CAT
LAUNDROMAT

from
Over the River and Through the Wood

Over the river, and through the wood,
To grandfather's house we go;
The horse knows the way
To carry the sleigh,
Through the white and drifted snow.

Over the river and through the wood—
Oh, how the wind does blow!
It stings the toes,
And bites the nose,
As over the ground we go.

Over the river and through the wood—
To have a first-rate play.
Hear the bells ring,
"Ting-a-ling-ding!"
Hurrah for Thanksgiving Day!

Over the river and through the wood,
And straight through the barnyard gate.
We seem to go
Extremely slow—
It is so hard to wait!

Over the river and through the wood
Trot fast my dapple gray!
Spring over the ground
Like a hunting hound!
For 'tis Thanksgiving Day.

Over the river and through the wood—
Now grandmother's cap I spy!
Hurrah for the fun!
Is the pudding done?
Hurrah for the pumpkin-pie!

LYDIA MARIA CHILD

All in a Word

T for time to be together,
turkey, talk, and tangy weather.

H for harvest stored away,
home, and hearth, and holiday.

A for autumn's frosty art,
and abundance in the heart.

N for neighbors, and November,
nice things, new things to remember.

K for kitchen, kettles' croon,
kith and kin expected soon.

S for sizzles, sights, and sounds,
and something special that abounds.

That spells THANKS—for joy in living
and a jolly good Thanksgiving.

AILEEN FISHER

ABC Song

A, B, C, D, E, F, G,
H, I, J, K, L-M-N-O-P,
Q, R, S and T, U, V,
W, X, and Y, and Z.

Now I know my ABC's,
Next time won't you sing with me?

ANONYMOUS

A Was Once an Apple Pie

A was once an apple pie,
Pidy,
Widy,
Tidy,
Pidy,
Nice Insidy,
Apple pie!

B was once a little bear,
Beary,
Wary,
Hairy,
Beary,
Taky cary,
Little bear!

E was once a little eel,
Eely,
Weely,
Peely,
Eely,
Twirly, tweely,
Little eel!

F was once a little fish,
Fishy,
Wishy,
Squishy,
Fishy,
In a dishy,
Little fish!

I was once a bottle of ink,
Inky,
Dinky,
Thinky,
Inky,
Blacky minky,
Bottle of ink!

J was once a jar of jam,
Jammy,
Mammy,
Clammy,
Jammy,
Sweety, swammy,
Jar of jam!

C was one a little cake,
    Caky,
    Baky,
    Maky,
    Caky,
    Take caky,
    Little cake!

D was once a little doll,
    Dolly,
    Molly,
    Polly,
    Nolly,
    Nursy dolly,
    Little doll!

G was once a little goose,
    Goosy,
    Moosy,
    Boosy,
    Goosy,
    Waddly-woosy,
    Little goose!

H was once a little hen,
    Henny,
    Chenny,
    Tenny,
    Henny,
    Eggsy-any,
    Little hen?

K was once a little kite,
    Kity,
    Whity,
    Flighty,
    Kity,
    Out of sighty,
    Little kite!

L was once a little lark,
    Larky,
    Marky,
    Harky,
    Larky,
    In the parky,
    Little lark!

M was once a little mouse,
Mousy,
Bousy,
Sousy,
Mousy,
In the housy,
Little mouse!

N was once a little needle,
Needly,
Tweedly,
Threedly,
Needly,
Wisky, wheedly,
Little needle!

Q was once a little quail,
Quaily,
Faily,
Daily,
Quaily,
Stumpy-taily,
Little quail!

R was once a little rose,
Rosy,
Posy,
Nosy,
Rosy,
Blows-y, grows-y,
Little rose!

U was once a little urn,
Urny,
Burny,
Turny,
Urny,
Bubbly, burny,
Little urn!

V was once a little vine,
Viny,
Winy,
Twiny,
Viny,
Twisty-twiny,
Little vine!

was once a little owl,
Owly,
Prowly,
Howly,
Owly,
Browny fowly,
Little owl!

P was once a little pump,
Plumpy,
Slumpy,
Flumpy,
Pumpy,
Dumpy, thumpy,
Little pump!

was once a little shrimp,
Shrimpy,
Nimpy,
Flimpy,
Shrimpy,
Jumpy, jimpy,
Little shrimp!

T was once a little thrush,
Thrushy,
Hushy,
Bushy,
Thrushy,
Flitty, flushy,
Little thrush!

was once a whale,
Whaly,
Scaly,
Shaly,
Whaly,
Tumbly-taily,
Mighty whale!

X was once a great king Xerxes,
Xerxy,
Perxy,
Turxy,
Xerxy,
Linky, lurxy,
Great King Xerxes!

Y was once a little yew,
      Yewdy,
      Fewdy,
      Crudy,
      Yewdy,
   Growdy, grewdy,
   Little yew!

Z was once a piece of zinc,
      Tinky,
      Winky,
      Blinky,
      Tinky,
   Tinkly minky,
   Piece of zinc!

EDWARD LEAR

Counting

1-2
I love you.

3-4
I love you more.

5-6
Fiddlesticks!

7-8
I think you're great.

9-10
Let's
start counting
all over
again.

LEE BENNETT HOPKINS

Five Little Monsters

Five little monsters
By the light of the moon
Stirring pudding with
A wooden pudding spoon.
The first one says,
"It musn't be runny."
The second one says,
"That would make it taste funny."
The third one says,
"It mustn't be lumpy."
The fourth one says,
"That would make me grumpy."
The fifth one smiles,
Hums a little tune,
And licks all the drippings
From the wooden pudding spoon.

EVE MERRIAM

Moon Pudding

9 Cups of Morning Dew
1¾ ounce Toads Breath
6 powdered Mouse Whiskers
3 lbs. Gr____ Chee__
1 ½p____ ___rs Milk
Stir vigorously by a.   Serves 5
full moon.

Five Little Chickens

Said the first little chicken,
  With a queer little squirm,
"I wish I could find
  A fat little worm."

Said the next little chicken,
  With an odd little shrug,
"I wish I could find
  A fat little slug."

Said the third little chicken,
  With a sharp little squeal,
"I wish I could find
  Some nice yellow meal."

Said the fourth little chicken,
  With a small sigh of grief,
"I wish I could find
  A little green leaf."

Said the fifth little chicken,
  With a faint little moan,
"I wish I could find
  A wee gravel stone."

"Now, see here," said the mother,
  From the green garden patch,
"If you want any breakfast,
  Just come here and scratch."

ANONYMOUS

Seven Little Rabbits

Seven little rabbits
Walkin' down the road
Walkin' down the road
Seven little rabbits
Walkin' down the road
To call on old friend toad.

One little rabbit
Said he was tired
Walkin' down the road
Walkin' down the road
One little rabbit
Said he was tired
Walkin' down the road
To call on old friend toad.

Six little rabbits
Walkin' down the road
Walkin' down the road
Six little rabbits
Walkin' down the road
To call on old friend toad.

One little rabbit
Said he was tired
Walkin' down the road
Walkin' down the road
One little rabbit
Said he was tired
Walkin' down the road
To call on old friend toad.

So
Six little rabbits
Turned around
Until they found
Down in the ground
A hole
Built by a mole.

So
Seven little rabbits
Turned around
Until they found
Down in the ground
A hole
Built by a mole.

Seven little rabbits
Went down the hole
Built by the mole
Down in the ground
Until they found
A den.

Then
The seventh little rabbit
Went to sleep—
Now don't say "Peep"—
He's tucked in bed
And now instead

Six little rabbits
Went down the hole
Built by the mole
Down in the ground
Until they found
A den.

Then
The sixth little rabbit
Went to sleep—
Now don't say "Peep"—
He's tucked in bed
And now instead

Five little rabbits
Walkin' down the road
Walkin' down the road
Five little rabbits
Walkin' down the road
To call on old friend toad.

One little rabbit
Said he was tired
Walkin' down the road
Walkin' down the road
One little rabbit
Said he was tired
Walkin' down the road
To call on old friend toad.

So
Five little rabbits
Turned around
Until they found
Down in the ground
A hole
Built by a mole.

Four little rabbits
Walkin' down the road
Walkin' down the road
Four little rabbits
Walkin' down the road
To call on old friend toad.

One little rabbit
Said he was tired
Walkin' down the road
Walkin' down the road
One little rabbit
Said he was tired
Walkin' down the road
To call on old friend toad.

Five little rabbits
Went down the hole
Built by the mole
Down in the ground
Until they found
A den.

Then
The fifth little rabbit
Went to sleep—
Now don't say "Peep"—
He's tucked in bed
And now instead

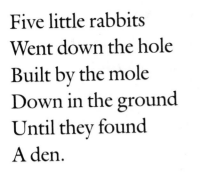

So
Four little rabbits
Turned around
Until they found
Down in the ground
A hole
Built by a mole.

Four little rabbits
Went down the hole
Built by the mole
Down in the ground
Until they found
A den.

Then
The fourth little rabbit
Went to sleep—
Now don't say "Peep"—
He's tucked in bed
And now instead

Three little rabbits
Walkin' down the road
Walkin' down the road
Three little rabbits
Walkin' down the road
To call on old friend toad.

One little rabbit
Said he was tired
Walkin' down the road
Walkin' down the road
One little rabbit
Said he was tired
Walkin' down the road
To call on old friend toad.

So
Three little rabbits
Turned around
Until they found
Down in the ground
A hole
Built by a mole.

Two little rabbits
Walkin' down the road
Walkin' down the road
Two little rabbits
Walkin' down the road
To call on old friend toad.

One little rabbit
Said he was tired
Walkin' down the road
Walkin' down the road
One little rabbit
Said he was tired
Walkin' down the road
To call on old friend toad.

Three little rabbits
Went down the hole
Built by the mole
Down in the ground
Until they found
A den.

Then
The third little rabbit
Went to sleep—
Now don't say "Peep"—
He's tucked in bed
And now instead

So
Two little rabbits
Turned around
Until they found
Down in the ground
A hole
Built by a mole.

Two little rabbits
Went down the hole
Built by the mole
Down in the ground
Until they found
A den.

Then
The second little rabbit
Went to sleep—
Now don't say "Peep"—
He's tucked in bed
And now instead

One little rabbit
Walkin' down the road
Walkin' down the road
One little rabbit
Walkin' down the road
To call on old friend toad.

One little rabbit
Said he was tired
Walkin' down the road
Walkin' down the road
One little rabbit
Said he was tired
Walkin' down the road
To call on old friend toad.

So
One little rabbit
Turned around
Until he found
Down in the ground
A hole
Built by a mole.

MRS RABBITS
CARROT CAKE

MOLE HOLE

❖ 44 ❖

The one little rabbit
Went down the hole
Built by the mole
Down in the ground
Until he found
A den.

Then
The first little rabbit
Who was also the last
Went to sleep—
Now don't say "Peep"—
He's tucked in bed
And now instead
Of walkin' down the road
Of walkin' down the road

The first little rabbit
Dreamed a dream
And to him it seemed
All in a blur
As if there were

Seven little rabbits
Walkin' down the road
Walkin' down the road
Seven little rabbits
Walkin' down the road
To call on old friend toad.

JOHN BECKER

Old Noah's Ark

Old Noah once he built an ark,
And patched it up with hickory bark.
He anchored it to a great big rock,
And then he began to load his stock.

The animals went in one by one,
The elephant chewing a carroway bun.

The animals went in two by two,
The crocodile and the kangaroo.

The animals went in three by three,
The tall giraffe and the tiny flea.

The animals went in four by four,
The hippopatomus stuck in the door.

The animals went in five by five,
The bees mistook the bear for a hive.

The animals went in six by six,
The monkey was up to his usual tricks.

The animals went in seven by seven,
Said the ant to the elephant, "Who are you shovin'?"

The animals went in eight by eight,
Some were early and some were late.

The animals went in nine by nine,
They all formed fours and marched in a line.

The animals went in ten by ten,
If you want any more, you can read it again.

FOLK RHYME

Mr. Finney's Turnip

Mr. Finney had a turnip
   And it grew behind the barn;
And it grew and it grew,
   And that turnip did no harm.

There it grew and it grew
   Till it could grow no longer;
Then his daughter Lizzie picked it
   And put it in the cellar.

There it lay and it lay
   Till it began to rot;
And his daughter Susie took it
   And put it in the pot.

And they boiled it and boiled it
   As long as they were able;
And then his daughters took it
   And put it on the table.

Mr. Finney and his wife
   They sat them down to sup;
And they ate and they ate
   And they ate that turnip up.

ANONYMOUS

Poor Old Lady

Poor old lady, she swallowed a fly.
I don't know why she swallowed a fly.
Poor old lady, I think she'll die.

Poor old lady, she swallowed a spider.
It squirmed and wriggled and turned inside her.
She swallowed the spider to catch the fly.
I don't know why she swallowed a fly.
Poor old lady, I think she'll die.

Poor old lady, she swallowed a bird.
How absurd! She swallowed a bird.
She swallowed the bird to catch the spider,
She swallowed the spider to catch the fly.
I don't know why she swallowed a fly.
Poor old lady, I think she'll die.

Poor old lady, she swallowed a cat.
Think of that! She swallowed a cat.
She swallowed the cat to catch the bird,
She swallowed the bird to catch the spider,
She swallowed the spider to catch the fly.
I don't know why she swallowed a fly.
Poor old lady, I think she'll die.

Poor old lady, she swallowed a dog.
She went the whole hog when she swallowed the dog.
She swallowed the dog to catch the cat,
She swallowed the cat to catch the bird,
She swallowed the bird to catch the spider,
She swallowed the spider to catch the fly.
I don't know why she swallowed a fly.
Poor old lady, I think she'll die.

Poor old lady, she swallowed a cow.
I don't know how she swallowed the cow.
She swallowed the cow to catch the dog,
She swallowed the dog to catch the cat,
She swallowed the cat to catch the bird,
She swallowed the bird to catch the spider,
She swallowed the spider to catch the fly.
I don't know why she swallowed a fly.
Poor old lady, I think she'll die.

Poor old lady, she swallowed a horse.
She died, of course.

ANONYMOUS

The Mouse, the Frog, and the Little Red Hen

Once a Mouse, a Frog, and a Little Red Hen
    Together kept a house;
The Frog was the laziest of frogs,
    And lazier still was the Mouse.

The work all fell on the Little Red Hen,
    Who had to get the wood,
And build the fires, and scrub, and cook,
    And sometimes hunt the food.

One day, as she went scratching round,
    She found a bag of rye;
Said she, "Now, who will make some bread?"
    Said the lazy Mouse, "Not I."

"Nor I," croaked the Frog, as he drowsed in the shade.
    Red Hen made no reply,
But flew around with bowl and spoon,
    And mixed and stirred the rye.

"Who'll make the fire to bake the bread?"
    Said the Mouse again, "Not I,"
And, scarcely op'ning his sleepy eyes,
    Frog made the same reply.

The Little Red Hen said never a word,
    But a roaring fire she made;
And while the bread was baking brown,
    "Who'll set the table?" she said.

"Not I," said the sleepy Frog with a yawn;
    "Nor I," said the Mouse again.
So the table she set, and the bread put on,
    "Who'll eat this bread?" said the Hen.

"I will!" cried the Frog. "And I!" squeaked the Mouse,
    As they near the table drew:
"Oh, no, you won't!" said the Little Red Hen,
    And away with the loaf she flew.

ANONYMOUS

The House That Jack Built

This is the house that Jack built.
This is the malt
That lay in the house that Jack built.

This is the rat,
That ate the malt,
That lay in the house that Jack built.

This is the cat,
That killed the rat,
That ate the malt,
That lay in the house that Jack built.

This is the dog,
That worried the cat,
That killed the rat,
That ate the malt,
That lay in the house that Jack built.

This is the cow with the crumpled horn,
That tossed the dog,
That worried the cat,
That killed the rat,
That ate the malt,
That lay in the house that Jack built.

This is the maiden all forlorn,
That milked the cow with the crumpled horn,
That tossed the dog,
That worried the cat,
That killed the rat,
That ate the malt,
That lay in the house that Jack built.

This is the man all tattered and torn,
That kissed the maiden all forlorn,
That milked the cow with the crumpled horn,
That tossed the dog,
That worried the cat,
That killed the rat,
That ate the malt,
That lay in the house that Jack built.

This is the priest all shaven and shorn,
That married the man all tattered and torn,
That kissed the maiden all forlorn,
That milked the cow with the crumpled horn,
That tossed the dog,
That worried the cat,
That killed the rat,
That ate the malt,
That lay in the house that Jack built.

FOLLOW ME

This is the cock that crowed in the morn,
That waked the priest all shaven and shorn,
That married the man all tattered and torn,
That kissed the maiden all forlorn,
That milked the cow with the crumpled horn,
That tossed the dog,
That worried the cat,
That killed the rat,
That ate the malt,
That lay in the house that Jack built.

This is the farmer sowing his corn,
That kept the cock that crowed in the morn,
That waked the priest all shaven and shorn,
That married the man all tattered and torn,
That kissed the maiden all forlorn,
That milked the cow with the crumpled horn,
That tossed the dog,
That worried the cat,
That killed the rat,
That ate the malt,
That lay in the house that Jack built.

ANONYMOUS

The Walrus and the Carpenter

'The sun was shining on the sea,
    Shining with all his might:
He did his very best to make
    The billows smooth and bright—
And this very odd, because it was
    The middle of the night.

The moon was shining sulkily,
    Because she thought the sun
Had got no business to be there
    After the day was done—
'It's very rude of him,' she said,
    'To come and spoil the fun!'

The sea was wet as wet could be,
    The sands were dry as dry.
You could not see a cloud, because
    No cloud was in the sky:
No birds were flying overhead—
    There were no birds to fly.

The Walrus and the Carpenter
    Were walking close at hand:
They wept like anything to see
    Such quantities of sand:
'If this were only cleared away,'
    They said, 'it *would* be grand!'

'If seven maids with seven mops
    Swept it for half a year,
Do you suppose,' the Walrus said,
    'That they could get it clear?'
'I doubt it,' said the Carpenter,
    And shed a bitter tear.

MORE

'O Oysters, come and walk with us!'
    The Walrus did beseech.
'A pleasant walk, a pleasant talk,
    Along the briny beach:
We cannot do with more than four,
    To give a hand to each.'

The eldest Oyster looked at him,
    But never a word he said:
The eldest Oyster winked his eye,
    And shook his heavy head—
Meaning to say he did not choose
    To leave the oyster-bed.

But four young Oysters hurried up,
    All eager for the treat:
Their coats were brushed, their faces washed,
    Their shoes were clean and neat—
And this was odd, because, you know,
    They hadn't any feet.

Four other Oysters followed them,
    And yet another four;
And thick and fast they came at last,
    And more, and more, and more—
All hopping through the frothy waves,
    And scrambling to the shore.

The Walrus and the Carpenter
    Walked on a mile or so,
And then they rested on a rock
    Conveniently low:
And all the little Oysters stood
    And waited in a row.

'The time has come,' the Walrus said,
    'To talk of many things:
Of shoes—and ships—and sealing-wax—
    Of cabbages—and kings—
And why the sea is boiling hot—
    And whether pigs have wings.'

'But wait a bit,' the Oysters cried,
    'Before we have our chat;
For some of us are out of breath,
    And all of us are fat!'
'No hurry,' said the Carpenter.
    They thanked him much for that.

'A loaf of bread,' the Walrus said,
    'Is what we chiefly need:
Pepper and vinegar besides
    Are very good indeed—
Now if you're ready, Oysters dear,
    We can begin to feed.'

'But not on us!' the Oysters cried,
    Turning a little blue.
'After such kindness that would be
    A dismal thing to do!'
'The night is fine,' the Walrus said.
    'Do you admire the view?'

'It was so kind of you to come!
    And you are very nice!'
The Carpenter said nothing but
    'Cut us another slice.
I wish you were not quite so deaf—
    I've had to ask you twice!'

'It seems a shame,' the Walrus said,
  'To play them such a trick.
After we've brought them out so far,
  And made them trot so quick!'
The Carpenter said nothing but
  'The butter's spread too thick!'

'I weep for you,' the Walrus said:
  'I deeply sympathize.'
With sobs and tears he sorted out
  Those of the largest size,
Holding his pocket-handkerchief
  Before his streaming eyes.

'O Oysters,' said the Carpenter,
  'You've had a pleasant run!
Shall we be trotting home again?'
  But answer came there none—
And this was scarcely odd, because
  They'd eaten every one.

LEWIS CARROLL

Snow

We'll play in the snow
And stray in the snow
And stay in the snow
In a snow-white park.
We'll clown in the snow
And frown in the snow
Fall down in the snow
Till it's after dark.
We'll cook snow pies
In a big snow pan.
We'll make snow eyes
In a round snow man.
We'll sing snow songs
And chant snow chants
And roll in the snow
In our fat snow pants.
And when it's time to go home to eat
We'll have snow toes
On our frosted feet.

KARLA KUSKIN

Hanukkah Candles

Light a candle, then one more.
Add another nightly,
Soon you will have three and four
Burning, burning brightly.
Five, six, seven, eight ablaze,
Happiest of sights,
Shining through the holidays
A Festival of Lights.

MARGARET HILLERT

For Allan

Who wanted to see how I wrote a poem

Among these mountains, do you know.
I have a farm, and on it grow
A thousand lovely Christmas trees.
I'd like to send you one of these,
But it's against the laws.
A man may give a little boy
A book, a useful knife, a toy,
Or even a rhyme like this by me
(I wrote it just like this you see),
But nobody may give a tree
Excepting Santa Claus.

ROBERT FROST

Christmas Is Coming

Christmas is coming. The geese are getting fat.
Please to put a penny in the old man's hat.
If you haven't got a penny, a ha'penny will do,
If you haven't got a ha'penny, God bless you.

ANONYMOUS

No Need to Light a Night Light

You've no need to light a night light
On a light night like tonight,
For a night light's light's a slight light,
And tonight's a night that's light.

When a night's light, like tonight's light,
It is really not quite right
To light night lights with their slight-lights
On a light night like tonight.

ANONYMOUS

A Visit from St. Nicholas

'Twas the night before Christmas, when all through the house
Not a creature was stirring, not even a mouse;
The stockings were hung by the chimney with care,
In hopes that St. Nicholas soon would be there;
The children were nestled all snug in their beds,
While visions of sugarplums danced in their heads;
And mamma in her 'kerchief, and I in my cap,
Had just settled our brains for a long winter's nap—
When out on the lawn there arose such a clatter,
I sprang from my bed to see what was the matter.
Away to the window I flew like a flash,
Tore open the shutters, and threw up the sash,
The moon, on the breast of the new-fallen snow,
Gave the lustre of midday to objects below;
When, what to my wondering eyes should appear,
But a miniature sleigh and eight tiny reindeer,
With a little old driver, so lively and quick,
I knew in a moment it must be St. Nick.
More rapid than eagles his coursers they came,
And he whistled, and shouted, and called them by name:
"Now, *Dasher!* now, *Dancer!* now, *Prancer* and *Vixen!*
On, *Comet!* on, *Cupid!* on *Donder* and *Blitzen!*'
To the top of the porch! to the top of the wall!
Now dash away! dash away! dash away all!
As dry leaves that before the wild hurricane fly,
When they meet with an obstacle, mount to the sky;
So up to the house-top the coursers they flew
With the sleigh full of toys, and St. Nicholas too.

Continued→

And then, in a twinkling, I heard on the roof
The prancing and pawing of each little hoof—
As I drew in my head, and was turning around,
Down the chimney St. Nicholas came with a bound.
He was dressed all in fur, from his head to his foot,
And his clothes were all tarnished with ashes and soot;
A bundle of toys he had flung on his back,
And he looked like a pedlar just opening his pack.
His eyes—how they twinkled; his dimples, how merry!
His cheeks were like roses, his nose like a cherry!
His droll little mouth was drawn up like a bow,
And the beard of his chin was as white as the snow;
The stump of a pipe he held tight in his teeth,
And the smoke it encircled his head like a wreath;
He had a broad face and a round little belly
That shook, when he laughed, like a bowl full of jelly.
He was chubby and plump, a right jolly old elf,
And I laughed when I saw him, in spite of myself;
A wink of his eye and a twist of his head
Soon gave me to know I had nothing to dread;
He spoke not a word, but went straight to his work,
And filled all the stockings; then turned with a jerk,
And laying his finger aside of his nose,
And giving a nod, up the chimney, he rose;
He sprang to his sleigh, to his team gave a whistle,
And away they all flew like the down of a thistle.
But I heard him exclaim, ere he drove out of sight,
"Happy Christmas to all, and to all a good night!"
CLEMENT CLARKE MOORE

Thank you S.C.

Jump—Jump—Jump

Jump—jump—jump—
  Jump away
From this town into
  The next, to-day.

Jump—jump—jump—
  Jump over the moon;
Jump all the morning,
  And all the noon.

Jump—jump—jump—
  Jump all night;
Won't our mothers
  Be in a fright?

Jump—jump—jump—
  Over the sea;
What wonderful wonders
  We shall see.

Jump—jump—jump—
  Jump far away;
And all come home
  Some other day.

KATE GREENAWAY

A House

Everyone has a house,
        a house,
everyone has a house.
The bear has a cave,
the bird a nest,
the mole a hole,
but what is best
is a house like ours
      with windows and doors
      and rugs and floors.

Everyone has a house,
        a house,
everyone has a house.

CHARLOTTE ZOLOTOW

Wee Willie Winkie

Wee Willie Winkie runs through the town,
Upstairs and downstairs in his nightgown,
Rapping at the window, crying through the lock,
"Are the children in their beds?
For now it's eight o'clock."

MOTHER GOOSE

Good Night

Goodnight Mommy
Goodnight Dad

I kiss them as I go

Goodnight Teddy
Goodnight Spot

The moonbeams call me so

I climb the stairs
Go down the hall
And walk into my room

My day of play is ending
But my night of sleep's in bloom

NIKKI GIOVANNI

Bed Mate

Whenever lightning strikes at night
    And thunder starts to boom,
My little sister, Ann Marie,
    Comes creeping to my room.

I don't mind moving over
    So there's room for Ann Marie,
I just wish that she would not put
    Her cold feet next to me!

CONSTANCE ANDREA KEREMES

Diddle, Diddle, Dumpling

Diddle, diddle, dumpling, my son John
Went to bed with his stockings on;
One shoe off, and one shoe on,
Diddle, diddle, dumpling, my son John.

MOTHER GOOSE

Far Away

How far, today,
Is far away?
It's farther now than I can say,
It's farther now than you can say.
It's farther now than who can say,
It's very *very* far away:
You'd better better better play,
You'd better stay and play today.
Okay…okay…okay.

DAVID MC CORD

First Star

Star light, star bright,
First star I've seen tonight!
I wish I may, I wish I might
Have the wish I wish tonight.

ANONYMOUS

Prayer

Now I lay me down to sleep,
I pray Thee, Lord, Thy child to keep:
Thy love guard me through the night
And wake me with the morning light.

ANONYMOUS

Happy Thought

The world is so full of a number of things,
I'm sure we should all be as happy as kings.

ROBERT LOUIS STEVENSON

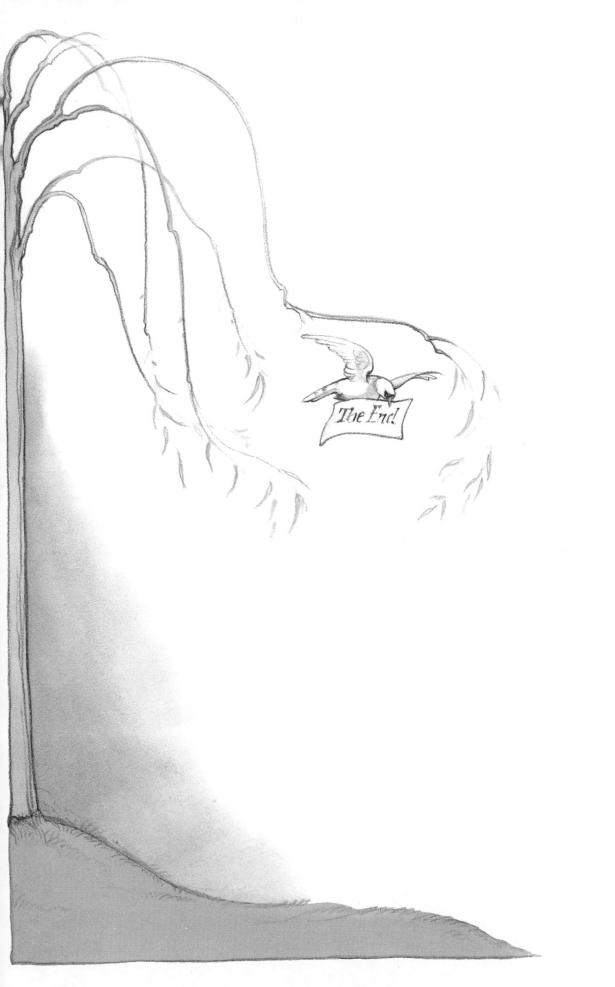

The End

INDEX

INDEX OF TITLES

INDEX OF AUTHORS

INDEX OF FIRST LINES

ACKNOWLEDGEMENTS

Every effort has been made to trace the ownership of all copyrighted material and to secure the necessary permissions to reprint these selections. In the event of any question arising as to the use of any material, the editor and the publisher, while expressing regret for any inadvertent error, will be happy to make the necessary correction in future printings.

Thanks are due to the following for permission to reprint the copyrighted materials listed below:

Abingdon Press, for "Halloween" from *I Rode The Black Horse Far Away* by Ivy O. Eastwick. Copyright © 1960 by Abingdon Press. Used by permission.

John Becker for "Seven Little Rabbits" from *New Feathers for the Old Goose.* Published by Pantheon Books, Inc. Copyright © 1956 by John Becker.

Curtis Brown, Ltd., for "Counting" by Lee Bennett Hopkins. Copyright © 1987 by Lee Bennett Hopkins. "Munching Peaches" by Lee Bennett Hopkins. Copyright © 1984 by Lee Bennett Hopkins. Used by permission of Curtis Brown, Ltd.

Aileen Fisher for "The Handiest Nose." Used by permission of the author, who controls all rights.

HarperCollins for "Spring Again." Copyright © 1964 by Karla Kuskin. "Catherine." Copyright © 1958 by Karla Kuskin. "Snow." Copyright © 1968 by Karla Kuskin from *Dogs & Dragons Trees & Dreams: A Collection of Poems* by Karla Kuskin. "Tommy" from *Bronzeville Boys and Girls* by Gwendolyn Brooks. Copyright © 1956 by Gwendolyn Brooks Blakely. "Moonstruck" from *Out in the Dark and Daylight* by Aileen Fisher. Copyright © 1980 by Aileen Fisher; "Limerick" from *A Book of Pigericks* by Arnold Lobel. Copyright © 1983 by Arnold Lobel. "All in A Word" and "Easter's Coming" from *Skip Around the Year* by Aileen Fisher. Copyright © 1967 by Aileen Fisher (T. Y. Crowell). All reprinted by permission of HarperCollins.

Margaret Hillert for "Hanukkah." Used by permission of the author, who controls all rights.

Henry Holt & Company, Inc., for "For Allan" from *Robert Frost: Poetry and Prose*, edited by Edward Connery Lathem and Lawrence Thompson. Copyright 1972 by Holt, Rinehart & Winston, Inc. Reprinted by permission of Henry Holt & Company, Inc.

Constance Andrea Keremes for "Bed Mate." Used by permission of the author, who controls all rights.

Alfred A. Knopf, Inc., for "April Rain Song" from *The Dream Keeper and Other Poems* by Langston Hughes Copyright © 1932 by Alfred A. Knopf, Inc. and renewed 1960 by Langston Hughes. Reprinted by permission of Alfred A. Knopf, Inc.

Sandra Liatsos for "Sea Wave." Used by permission of the author, who controls all rights; "Wild Geese." Reprinted from *Ranger Rick*, April 1980, with permission from the pulisher, National Wildlife Federation, and the author.

Little, Brown & Company, Inc. for "The Pickety Fence" and "Far Away" from *One at a Time* by David McCord. Copyright 1952 by David McCord. Copyright © renewed 1980 by David McCord. Reprinted by permission of Little, Brown, Inc.

Beverly McLoughland for "Secret." Used by permission of the author, who controls all rights.

William Morrow & Company, Inc. for "Good Night" from *Vacation Time* by Nikki Giovanni. Copyright © 1980 by Nikki Giovanni. By permission of William Morrow & Company, Inc.

G. P. Putnam's Sons, for "The Picnic" from *Hop, Skip and Jump!* by Dorothy Aldis. Copyright © 1934 by Dorothy Aldis, copyright © renewed 1961 by Dorothy Aldis. Reprinted by permission of G. P. Putnam's Sons.

Marian Reiner for "Follow the Leader" from *The Wizard in the Well: Poems and Pictures* by Harry Behn. Copyright © 1956 by Harry Behn. Copyright © renewed 1984 by Alice Behn Goebel, Pamel Behn Adam, Peter Behn, and Prescott Behn. "Five Little Monsters" from *Blackberry Ink* by Eve Merriam. Copyright © 1985 by Eve Merriam. All rights reserved. "Look at That!" from *See My Lovely Poison Ivy* by Lilian Moore. Copyright © 1975 by Lilian Moore. All rights reserved. "Seaweed" from *Wide Awake and Other Poems* by Myra Cohn Livingston. Copyright © 1959 by Myra Cohn Livingston. "Will You?" from *The Birthday Cow* by Eve Merriam. Copyright © 1978 by Eve Merriam. All reprinted by permission of Marian Reiner for the authors.

Charlotte Zolotow for "A House." Used by permission of the author, who controls all rights.

Special thanks to Alan Benjamin and Grace D. Clarke of Simon & Schuster, Inc., for the tender care they have given to this volume.

Published by The Trumpet Club
666 Fifth Avenue, New York, New York 10103

Compilation and Introduction © 1988 by Lee Bennett Hopkins
Illustrations © 1988 by Hilary Knight

ISBN: 0-440-84670-6

This edition published by arrangement with Simon and Schuster Books for Young Readers, a division of Simon & Schuster, Inc.
Designed by Sylvia Frezzolini
Printed in the United States of America
October 1991

10 9 8 7 6 5 4 3 2 1
SEM

ANTHOLOGIST
Lee Bennett Hopkins

SAYS:

Among my fondest
memories are the times my
grandmother recited, from
memory, some wonderful
poems her mother had read
to her. Many of these same
verses are here in *Side by
Side*. It shows that good
poetry lasts *forever*! Thanks
grandma.

ILLUSTRATOR
Hilary Knight

SAYS:

One of the pleasures of my
childhood was having my
parents (artists Clayton
Knight and Katharine
Sturges) read aloud to my
brother and myself.

I can still recall my father's
spirited reciting of *I Went
to the Animal Fair*. It was,
therefore, a special treat to
find it included in this
collection.

So, *Side by Side*, let's
look, listen, and
have a lovely time.